SCI-FI TE███████

WHAT WOULD IT TAKE TO BUILD A

DEFLECTOR

SHIELD?

BY ROBERTA BAXTER

CAPSTONE PRESS
a capstone imprint

Capstone Captivate is published by Capstone Press, an imprint of Capstone.
1710 Roe Crest Drive
North Mankato, Minnesota 56003
www.capstonepub.com

Library of Congress Cataloging-in-Publication Data
Names: Baxter, Roberta, 1952- author.
Title: What would it take to build a deflector shield? / by Roberta Baxter.
Description: North Mankato, Minnesota : Capstone Press, 2020. | Series:
   Sci-fi tech | Includes bibliographical references and index. | Audience:
   Grades 4-6.
Identifiers: LCCN 2019029494 (print) | LCCN 2019029495 (ebook) | ISBN
   9781543591200 (hardcover) | ISBN 9781496666000 (paperback) | ISBN 9781543591293 (ebook)
Subjects: LCSH: Shielding (Electricity)--Juvenile literature. |
   Absorption--Juvenile literature. | Shields--Juvenile literature. |
   Electronic security systems--Juvenile literature.
Classification: LCC TK7867.8 .B39 2020 (print) | LCC TK7867.8 (ebook) |
   DDC 629.47/2--dc23
LC record available at https://lccn.loc.gov/2019029494
LC ebook record available at https://lccn.loc.gov/2019029495

Image Credits
Alamy: Ronald Grant Archive, 6; iStockphoto: liuzishan, 10; Newscom: Larry Downing/Reuters, 14; Science Source: Jeff Huang, 26; Shutterstock Images, 3Dsculptor, 25, Algol, 21, Anton Shahrai, cover (earth), camilkuo, 5, Dima Zel, 22–23, Jurik Peter, 8–9, ktsdesign, 17, Levchenko Ilia, cover (shield), Rocksweeper, 18, seveniwe, 13, solarseven, 29, Triff, 11
Design Elements: Shutterstock Images

Editorial Credits
Editor: Arnold Ringstad; Designer: Laura Graphenteen

All internet sites appearing in back matter were available and accurate when this book was sent to press.

Printed in the United States of America.
PA99

TABLE OF CONTENTS

WORDS IN BOLD ARE IN THE GLOSSARY.

CHAPTER ONE

PROTECTED BY ENERGY

Two spaceships zoom toward each other. One shoots a beam of light at the other. The beam is an energy weapon. It streaks through space. It gets close to its target. But the other ship has a glowing bubble around it. The beam bounces off. It does not harm the ship. The attacking ship tries again. This time it launches a bomb. The bomb hits the bubble and explodes. The ship inside the bubble is unharmed.

The glowing bubble is a deflector shield. This shield provides protection. Deflector shields are made of energy. They block weapons. They also protect against other dangers in space, such as **radiation**. This is an invisible energy. It comes from stars and other objects in space. Radiation can make people sick. It may make space travel dangerous.

FUN FACT

Deflector shields are sometimes called force fields.

Space battles in science fiction often have energy weapons and deflector shields.

Today deflector shields are found only in science fiction. We find them in movies and books. These shields do not have solid science behind them. But scientists are studying how real shields might work. Could we make a deflector shield in real life?

Spaceships in the *Star Trek* series often have deflector shields.

CHAPTER TWO

WHAT IS A DEFLECTOR SHIELD?

In science-fiction stories, deflector shields protect against enemy weapons. They block weapons made of energy, such as **lasers**. Lasers are tight beams of light. The shields also block weapons that are objects, such as bombs. A spaceship uses a small deflector shield. A bigger shield can protect a city. A giant one can protect a whole planet.

In some movies deflector shields look like glowing bubbles. Other times the shields are invisible. They show up only when something hits them.

FUN FACT

Deflector shields are most famous from the *Star Wars* and *Star Trek* series.

Rocks drifting through space can be dangerous for spaceships.

Deflector shields protect against more than just weapons. Rocks and dust drift through space. These may not seem dangerous. But spaceships move at high speeds. At those speeds even dust could punch a hole through a ship. Deflector shields help. They block objects in the ship's path. This lets the ship zoom through space safely.

CHAPTER THREE

HOW WOULD A DEFLECTOR SHIELD WORK?

Deflector shields are made up of energy. The energy forms a big bubble. It wraps around the object that is being protected. It keeps weapons and other dangers away. How could these shields be made? Scientists have some ideas.

In science fiction, deflector shields protect cities of the future.

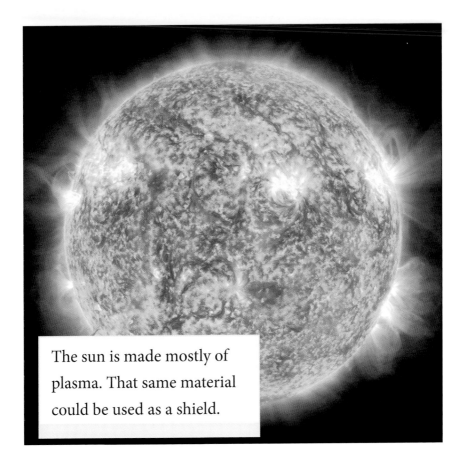

The sun is made mostly of plasma. That same material could be used as a shield.

One way is to use lasers to heat up air. The warm air would bend enemy lasers. Scientists also think that **plasma** might work. Plasma is a gas heated to very high temperatures. It bends a laser beam fired at it. However, there is one problem. If a spaceship released plasma, it would just spread all over. It would not protect anything. The ship would need a way to keep the plasma in a certain place.

Magnetic fields could help. Magnets can move plasma and hold it in place. The ship could use a magnetic field to shape the plasma into a shield. Then the plasma would protect the ship.

Magnets could have other uses in shields. A magnetic field itself could give protection from radiation. In *Star Trek*, deflector shields protect ships against radiation. In real life, a strong magnetic field could block radiation from entering a spaceship. It can keep the people inside safe.

FUN FACT

Scientists think that a magnetic field around 330 feet (100 meters) across could protect a spaceship.

EARTH'S MAGNETIC FIELD

Earth's magnetic field

radiation

sun

Earth has its own magnetic field. It protects us from radiation that comes from space.

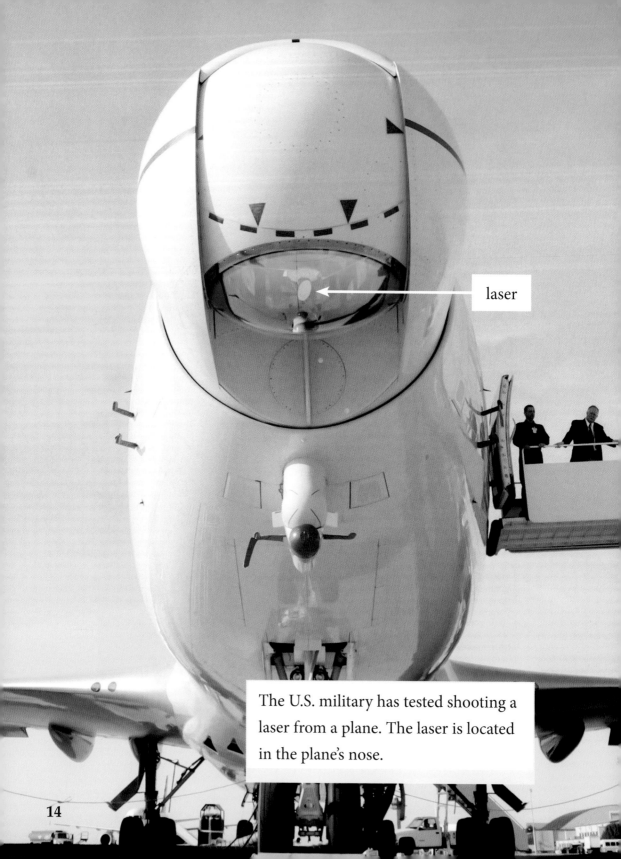

laser

The U.S. military has tested shooting a laser from a plane. The laser is located in the plane's nose.

CHAPTER FOUR

CURRENT TECH

People are figuring out ways to make deflector shields in real life. One company is testing a way to use lasers to make deflector shields. This deflector shield would protect airplanes from laser weapons shooting from the ground. The shield would work by heating up part of the **atmosphere**. The atmosphere is the blanket of air that surrounds Earth. It is made up of many layers. Warming up a layer of air can cause light to bend when it passes through. Lasers would bend because they are a form of light.

The airplane would fire lasers downward. This would heat the air between the plane and the laser weapon. When the enemy laser fired, it would bend away from the plane. The shield would keep the plane safe.

Deflector shields will be used against more than weapons. They will be used against radiation too. Like the beams that come from laser weapons, radiation is a kind of energy. Protecting against radiation will be important for future space travelers. Scientists are carefully studying how a magnetic shield might work. The key to this shield is **superconductors**. Superconductors are materials that can make strong magnetic fields. Some superconductors work only at very low temperatures. This would make them hard to use in space. The ship would need to carry very cold liquids to cool them. But newer superconductors work at higher temperatures. They will be easier to use in space.

SUPERCONDUCTORS IN TRAINS

Superconductors are used in some trains. These trains use them to create magnetic fields. The train and the track are magnetic. This lets the trains float above the track. These trains can reach very high speeds.

Superconductors create magnetic fields that can make things float. Magnetic fields could also act as shields.

Scientists have not built one of these shields yet. But they have studied how the shield would work using math. It would block much of the dangerous radiation in space. It would keep people safe.

Scientists want to protect tanks and other vehicles with plasma shields.

Scientists are looking into making deflector shields with plasma. This kind of shield would protect against some kinds of explosions. Explosions create a powerful blast of air. This blast can harm vehicles. The shield would have parts that sense when an explosion happened nearby. Then it would make a layer of plasma. The blast of air would hit the plasma. This would protect the vehicle. The shield would stay up for just a few moments. Scientists have made designs for this shield. But none have been built yet.

CHAPTER FIVE

WHAT TECH IS NEEDED?

Making plasma takes a lot of energy. So do powerful magnets and lasers. But making and storing lots of energy is hard. A machine that could make that power would be large and heavy. It would take up a lot of room in a spaceship. Finding a smaller, lighter energy source is an important step to building a deflector shield.

Plasma shields might work well. But people could not see through them. Scientists might have a way to fix this problem. The spaceship could use special cameras. The cameras could see kinds of light that people can't see. These kinds of light wouldn't be blocked by the plasma. People could look at the camera screens to see through the shield.

A small, lightweight energy source for making a deflector shield would let spaceships fly quickly.

Deflector shields in science fiction do not just block energy. They also block objects, from bombs to space dust. So far scientists don't have ideas for blocking objects. Scientists need to keep studying to think of ideas. Someday new technology might make these kinds of shields possible.

Deflector shields could be useful for protecting spaceships from dangerous objects in space.

Scientists think a laser deflector shield is possible. But they have not built one yet. They will need to build powerful lasers. They will need to figure out how to carefully aim the laser from a moving plane. Scientists think it could take until the 2050s to make a working shield.

CHAPTER SIX

WHAT COULD THE FUTURE LOOK LIKE?

Deflector shields would be useful for future space travel. Scientists are planning trips to Mars. This is a long trip. **Astronauts** would need to be in space for many months to get there. Radiation there is harmful. They would need shielding. A deflector shield that makes a magnetic field would keep them safe.

Once they get to Mars, the people would still need shields. The planet does not have a strong magnetic field. Dangerous radiation reaches the surface. Scientists think they could build a planetwide deflector shield. It would sit in space between Mars and the sun. It would block radiation from reaching the planet.

People traveling on
a spaceship to Mars
would need protection
from radiation.

Future deflector shields
could protect a large area.

Deflector shields could have many uses on Earth too. They could protect tanks, planes, and ships from enemy weapons. Shields could also protect people from natural disasters. People could go to a shelter protected by a shield. If an earthquake knocked a building down, they would be safe. It could block floodwaters. It could block lava from a volcano. A big shield could protect a whole city. A huge deflector shield could protect the planet. Huge rocks called **asteroids** float in space. Sometimes they hit planets. This can be very dangerous. A shield could block an asteroid that gets too close.

Scientists are studying new ways to make deflector shields work. Someday they might make shields that work like the ones in science fiction. Maybe you will travel on a spaceship with deflector shields. Imagine you are on a mission to Saturn's moons. You zoom through a group of asteroids. Your ship's deflector shield glows. When an asteroid hits, the space rock simply bounces off. Your ship is safe from harm.

Deflector shields could help with space travel. They could have many other uses too. What would you use a deflector shield for?

Deflector shields could protect Earth from asteroids.

GLOSSARY

asteroid (AS-tuh-roid)—a rock that floats in space

astronaut (AS-troh-not)—a person who goes into space

atmosphere (AT-muh-sfeer)—the air that surrounds Earth

laser (LAY-zur)—a device that creates a beam of tightly focused light

magnetic field (mag-NE-tik FEELD)—the area around something magnetic

plasma (PLAZ-muh)—what gas becomes when a lot of energy is run through it

radiation (ray-dee-AY-shun)—an invisible form of energy that can be harmful

superconductor (SOO-purr-con-duk-ter)—a material that pushes strongly against magnets when it is very cold

READ MORE

Adler, David A. *Solids, Liquids, Gases, and Plasma.* New York: Holiday House, 2019.

Spray, Sally. *Awesome Engineering Spacecraft.* North Mankato, MN: Capstone Publishers, 2018.

Weakland, Mark. *What Is Magnetism?* North Mankato, MN: Capstone Publishers, 2019.

INTERNET SITES

NASA: Mars for Kids
https://mars.nasa.gov/participate/funzone/

States of Matter: Plasma
https://www.sciencelearn.org.nz/resources/1499-states-of-matter

Time for Kids: What Are Magnets?
https://www.timeforkids.com/g34/what-are-magnets-2/

INDEX